Stephen HAWKING

Stephanie Sammartino McPherson

Twenty-First Century Books
Minneapolis

To my daughter Marianne, with love and with thanks for her enthusiasm and encouragement

The author would like to thank Robert H. Gowdy, Ph.D., chairman of the physics department at Virginia Commonwealth University, for reading the manuscript and for clarifying Hawking's ideas—especially on black holes, singularities, and virtual particles. Thanks also to Richard McPherson and to Marion and Angelo Sammartino for help and support. Finally, a big thank you to Marianne McPherson and to Jonathan Gardner for accompanying me to see Stephen Hawking receive the Smithsonian Institute's James Smithson Medal in Washington, D.C.

Twenty-First Century Books
A division of Lerner Publishing Group
241 First Avenue North
Minneapolis, MN 55401 U.S.A.

Website addresses: www.lernerbooks.com
www.biography.com

Library of Congress Cataloging-in-Publication Data

McPherson, Stephanie Sammartino.
    Stephen Hawking / by Stephanie Sammartino McPherson.
      p.   cm. — (Biography)
    Includes bibliographical references and index.
    ISBN-13: 978-0-8225-5950-4 (lib. bdg. : alk. paper)
    ISBN-10: 0-8225-5950-1 (lib. bdg. : alk. paper)
    1. Hawking, S. W. (Stephen W.) 2. Physicists—Great Britain—Biography. 3. Cosmology. 4. Big bang theory. 5. Black holes (Astronomy) 6. Space and time. I. Title. II. Series.
QC16.H33M37 2007
530.092—dc22   2005035147

Manufactured in the United States of America
1 2 3 4 5 6 – BP – 12 11 10 09 08 07

CONTENTS

Hawking (third from left) *appeared on* Star Trek: The Next Generation. *On the show, he played cards with actors portraying* Albert Einstein (left), *Data the robot, and Sir Isaac Newton* (right).

INTRODUCTION

The set of the television show *Star Trek: The Next Generation* buzzed with activity. The director was preparing to shoot another scene. But something was different this time. Instead of the regular actors, the attention focused on a slight man in a motorized wheelchair. He was almost completely paralyzed, but his blue eyes sparkled with interest as he took in the details of the starship *Enterprise*.

A throat operation eight years earlier had left the man unable to use his vocal cords. But people wished to speak with him. As the man's fingers squeezed a switch, he was able to select and spell words on a portable computer screen. The message he put together was fed into a voice synthesizer. In pleasant, artificial tones, the man "spoke," greeting people and expressing his appreciation of *Star Trek*.

In a way, the visitor had a great deal in common with the characters on the show. Their mission led them to distant parts of the galaxy. His adventures led him to new intellectual territory. The questions he asked sounded impossible. Did time and space have a beginning? What really happens when a dying star collapses? Are black holes gateways to other universes?

These were topics as strange as any tackled by *Star Trek*. Science fiction had met science fact in the person of world-famous physicist Stephen Hawking.

Even top scientists were sometimes hard-pressed to understand Hawking's complicated theories. That didn't stop him from writing a book about the universe for a popular audience. He felt that science was for everyone. He wanted his book to be sold even in airports, where hordes of travelers would see it.

Hawking's book, called *A Brief History of Time*, surpassed his wildest hopes. It became a runaway best seller and was translated into thirty languages. The publicity turned Hawking into a science superstar. When the producers of *Star Trek* learned he was visiting southern California, a great idea took shape in their minds. They invited Hawking to do more than simply visit their studio.

In July 1993, when viewers tuned in to the season finale of *Star Trek*, they witnessed an amusing card game. Data the robot, who could perform mathematical calculations at lightning speed, decided to pit his poker skills against the greatest geniuses of all time. He summoned up hologram images of Sir Isaac Newton, Albert Einstein, and Stephen Hawking. Enjoying it immensely, Hawking played himself.

The scene gently spoofed history's top physicists. When Hawking raised his bet by fifty dollars, Einstein was gleeful. He predicted that Stephen would lose the game. But Hawking had a surprise for his friends. Grinning, he used a mechanical device to display his winning cards. On that triumphant note, a red alert was sounded aboard the *Enterprise*. Data was forced to cancel the poker game, and Hawking's cameo role was over.

It was time to return to real life, and Hawking was ready. He once said that science fact can be even more astounding than science fiction. To prove his point, Hawking mentioned black holes. He felt they were stranger than any idea from a science fiction novel. As a professor at Cambridge University in England, Hawking has never stopped trying to solve the mystery of black holes—and of the entire universe.

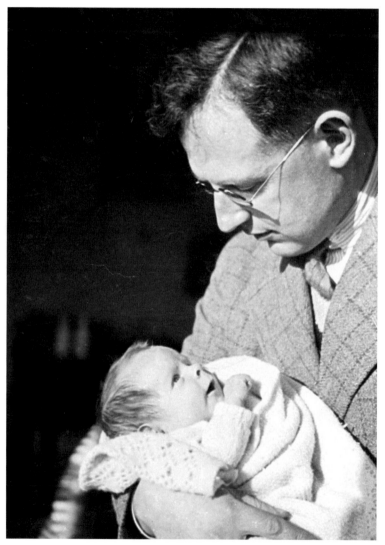

Frank Hawking, a doctor who researched diseases, holds his son, Stephen, born in 1942.

Chapter **ONE**

SCIENTIST IN THE MAKING

JANUARY 8, 1942, WAS SPECIAL FOR TWO IMPORTANT reasons. It marked the three-hundredth anniversary of the death of Galileo, who is often considered the world's first true scientist. By an interesting coincidence, it is also Stephen Hawking's birth date. He is quick to point out, however, that "two hundred thousand other babies were also born that day" and that he doesn't "know whether any of them were later interested in astronomy."

Great Britain was then in the middle of World War II (1939–1945). German air raids were a frightening and constant fact of life. Frank and Isobel Hawking wanted their son to be born someplace safe. Although they lived in London, the capital of

Britain, Isobel went to Cambridge as the time of the birth drew near. There, the anxious parents could be sure that no bombs would endanger their new baby. A special agreement between the warring countries guaranteed the safety of certain cities on both sides, and Cambridge was one of them.

Stephen was only two weeks old when his mother returned with him to London. Bombs still fell nightly, but the family decided to stick together and take their chances. One day, when Stephen was a toddler, Isobel returned home to discover that a German V-2—a huge rocket-propelled bomb—had exploded just several doors away from the Hawking residence. By that time, Stephen had a baby sister named Mary. Although both children had been out with their mother, Stephen's father had been home when the bomb hit. To Isobel's relief, he was not injured, and their house was only slightly damaged.

EARLY DAYS IN LONDON

The war had ended by the time four-year-old Stephen began school. He attended Bryon House, a school that stressed the natural approach to learning. Teachers expected their students to learn at their own pace, without being forced to repeat things over and over. Stephen took his time, only learning to read when he was eight years old. But he was bright and had a lively curiosity about all sorts of things.

Stephen with his sisters, Phillipa (center) *and Mary* (right)

Stephen's father was often away while his children were growing up. As a research doctor, he spent several months each year in Africa, where he investigated tropical diseases. Stephen, Mary, and Philippa, who was born two years after the war, became used to his absences. Despite his lengthy periods away, Frank Hawking had a strong influence on his son's life. Stephen took it for granted that he would have a career in science like his father. From his mother, he learned the importance of working for social justice and for peace. Nuclear weapons had been used to end World War II. Isobel Hawking wanted to ensure that such destructive forces were never used again.

Stephen at the age of eight

YOUNG EINSTEIN?

When Stephen was eight years old, the Hawkings moved to Saint Albans, a city about twenty miles (thirty-two kilometers) from London. Although his parents weren't wealthy, they managed to buy a large old house. Stephen loved his new bedroom. It was an easy leap from his window to the roof of the bicycle shed. He could come and go without using the front door. But that wasn't his only entry. According to his sister Mary, Stephen figured out eleven ways to get in and out of the house.

For several years, Stephen went to the local school at Saint Albans. His father hoped his son would eventually attend Westminster, one of the best schools in England. Unfortunately, thirteen-year-old Stephen was sick the day he was to take his scholarship test. Since he missed the exam and his parents could not send him to Westminster without financial aid, he had to stay at Saint Albans after all.

That was fine with Stephen. He liked Saint Albans School, although he only ranked in the middle of his class. Teachers complained that his handwriting was terrible, and even in his school uniform, he looked scruffy. But there was something special about Stephen. His schoolmates recognized it long before his teachers. Stephen was full of energy and ideas. Despite his average grades, his friends nicknamed him Einstein. Some friends thought he would match Einstein's achievements one day. Others thought that he didn't work hard enough to succeed. Two friends even bet a bag of candy over Stephen's future.

Perhaps Stephen shrugged the bet off. Perhaps he laughed. His parents certainly wouldn't have paid much attention. They cared little about what others thought. Considered a colorful pair, Frank and Isobel Hawking filled their home with books, paintings, and puzzling items from all over the world. They didn't worry much about peeling wallpaper or chipped plaster or worn carpeting. They kept bees in hives in the basement for honey, and at dinnertime they thought it was fine for family members to read separate books at the table. Even their vacations bore the Hawking stamp of uniqueness. They spent their holidays in a brightly painted camper in a field near the ocean.

When the Hawkings needed a new car, Stephen's father bought a prewar London taxicab with an open top. As if the taxi wasn't strange enough, Frank Hawking housed it in a military hut of corrugated (wavy) metal that Stephen helped his father assemble. "The neighbors were outraged," Stephen recalled. "but they couldn't stop us."

Stephen often wished he *could* stop his parents, though. He didn't really want to be different. A thin, eager boy, he was awkward at most sports, though he could run quickly. When he was excited, he spoke so rapidly his tongue seemed to trip over his own words. Like his father, he had a slight lisp—a problem pronouncing the *s* sound. His friends had a word for Stephen's speech. They called it Hawkingese. Stephen enjoyed going for long bicycle rides, listening to classical music, and talking about almost anything.

One of Stephen's favorite topics was astronomy, an interest shared by his whole family. Sometimes they would lie on the grass at night and take turns looking at the stars through a telescope. "Stephen always had a strong sense of wonder," his mother recalled. "I could see that the stars would draw him." Stephen remembers coming home one night after the street-

The Milky Way Galaxy captured Stephen's imagination.

lights had been turned off. The Milky Way Galaxy stretched across the sky in all its magnificence. He could only stare in awe.

Even in his early teens, Stephen wanted to know more about the universe. Some recent scientific observations seemed to indicate that the universe was getting bigger—that it was expanding almost like a balloon being blown up. Stephen found this hard to accept. He often discussed the issue with his friends. It seemed logical to him that the universe had always been the same. Maybe someday he could study the evidence himself.

Smaller problems fascinated Stephen too. He enjoyed taking things apart, such as clocks or small appliances, to see how they worked. The difficulty was putting them back together again! But Stephen was always up for a challenge.

He also liked to think up board games with his friends. Stephen, who invented most of the rules, enjoyed complicated games. His economics game had factories, railroads, and a stock market. His war game, based on World War II, had four thousand squares. Playing one of Stephen's games could easily take hours.

ENTHUSIASTIC BUILDER

Stephen made model airplanes too, though his enthusiasm usually exceeded his skill. "I was never very

Stephen had many friends in Saint Albans (below). *They made up games and built electronic devices.*

good with my hands," he admits. Luckily, his friend John McClenahan was more talented than Stephen. Even better, John's father had a well-equipped workshop. If Stephen's models looked a little strange, he didn't care. What mattered was how they worked.

Electronic devices were even more interesting than airplanes. They were fun to make and easier to control. But Stephen's clumsiness still caused problems. Once he gave himself a 500-volt shock trying to turn an old television set into an amplifier. Still, he managed to build a record player from cheap parts. Then he spent thirty-five shillings, a large sum for a teenage boy, to purchase his first long-playing record, a violin concerto by German composer Johannes Brahms.

One year later, Stephen and his group were ready for even bigger things. They used equipment from old telephone switchboards to build a computer. The boys called it LUCE, the Logical Uniselector Computing Engine. This was 1958, two decades before computers would begin to revolutionize communications. With the help of a math teacher, the boys worked on the computer for a month. They had to solder the electrical connections over and over again before it finally worked. The school magazine, the *Albanian*, and a local newspaper featured slightly humorous articles on the finished machine. According to the *Albanian*, the computer "answer[ed] some useless, though quite complex logical problems." It noted that the young inventors were already working on a machine that would add, subtract, multiply, and divide. True to this prediction, Stephen and his pals built an even better computer.

THE MOST BORING SUBJECT

In 1958 Stephen was sixteen years old. It was almost time to think of going to college. His father wanted him to go to Oxford University and study biology. Oxford sounded fine to Stephen. Biology did not. Stephen didn't want to become a doctor like his father. Instead, he was determined to study physics, the science that deals with matter and energy—even though he complained that it was the most boring subject in his school. Everything the teacher taught was too easy for him. But physics tugged at his imagination in a way that nothing else did.

Over and over again, Stephen and his father debated what he should do. Frank Hawking did not give up easily. He was afraid that physics would not prepare Stephen for a good job. Stephen was less concerned with money than with the discoveries he could make. Looking back on these years, he wrote that he wanted to understand "where we came from and why we were here. I wanted to fathom the far depths of the universe." The key to this ambition lay in physics, mathematics, and astronomy.

In the end, Stephen's determination won. He would apply for a scholarship in natural science at University College in Oxford. While his parents, sisters, and baby brother Edward spent a year in India, Stephen had to stay home and prepare for his two-day entrance test. Many students waited a year or two before applying to the university. Even the headmaster at Saint Albans said that seventeen-year-old Stephen was too young. But in March 1959, Stephen went to Oxford to take the test.

The exam was difficult, and Stephen felt he had done badly. Anxiously, he waited for word from the college. Ten days later, he received an invitation to come for another interview. Heartened, Stephen returned to Oxford. After only several days, he received a telegram announcing that he had received a scholarship. Stephen was going to Oxford after all.

Oxford University, which Stephen began to attend in 1959

Chapter **TWO**

A REASON TO LOOK FORWARD

IF **STEPHEN HAWKING HOPED TO BE CHALLENGED AT** Oxford, he was soon disappointed. The physics course was almost as easy as the one at Saint Albans. One day Stephen arrived in class without his assignment. The teacher in charge asked why Stephen hadn't completed the work. Stephen didn't reply. Instead, he opened his book and spent about twenty minutes pointing out all the mistakes on the pages. Another time three of his classmates found him reading a science fiction book the day some very difficult problems were due. They were shocked when Stephen said he hadn't started the assignment. They were even more surprised, however, when Stephen managed to complete nine problems before class. The trio had been working together for a week and had only managed to solve one.

Although Stephen did well academically, he was often lonely. None of his good friends from Saint Albans had come to Oxford, and he felt out of place. Things improved his second year when he decided to take up rowing. Stephen became the coxswain, or leader, of his crew. Stephen sat at one end of the boat, his face shaded by a straw hat. As he steered, he called out orders to the eight rowers. They were not a distinguished group of athletes, but that didn't matter to Stephen.

Sometimes there was ice on the river. Sometimes rain made huge puddles in the boat. Nothing kept the rowing crews from practicing. Even when the going

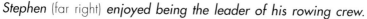

Stephen (far right) *enjoyed being the leader of his rowing crew.*

got rough or the river narrowed dangerously, Stephen steered onward. Splinters of wood were knocked from the boat, and the oars were damaged. Years later, a crew member recalled that Stephen "refused to give up on any of us, and somehow convinced us by the day of our first race that we were not quite so hopeless after all."

Rowing gave Stephen a new sense of belonging. He began to feel relaxed and happy at Oxford. Other students noticed his lively manner and sense of humor. Stephen was fun to be with, ready for adventure, and willing to share his passion for music and science fiction. He once estimated that he averaged only an hour a day on his coursework while he was at Oxford.

Aiming for Honors

But as graduation approached at the end of the third year, Stephen had to make some changes. Once again, he had to take an important test. This would determine what kind of degree he received from Oxford. Those who received the best scores would receive First degrees, the highest honor the university could bestow. Lesser scores would earn the graduates Second or Third degrees. Stephen needed a First. He had already been accepted to study for a doctorate at Cambridge University, Oxford's biggest rival—but only if he received top honors.

Stephen figured he would have no trouble when it came to doing the problems on his exam. What worried him were questions that tested his knowledge of the facts. Soon he was studying a whopping three hours daily. He felt relieved that he'd be given a choice of topics to write on. He hoped he could pick questions that didn't demand more than he knew.

Another concern marred Stephen's third year. One day, to his bewilderment, he had trouble rowing a racing boat. Although this seemed strange, Stephen had his upcoming exam to think about. Besides, he had always been a little bit clumsy. Then something more serious happened. He fell down the stairs in a university hall and hit his head. Stephen was stunned and confused. "Who am I?" he asked his worried friends.

Within hours Stephen's memory and mental clarity had returned. Still, the incident worried him so much that he decided to see a doctor. He wanted to make certain that he had not suffered brain damage. After a thorough checkup, the doctor told Stephen he was fine. But as an added reassurance, Stephen decided to take a test administered by Mensa, an organization for people who have especially high IQs. To his relief, Stephen scored extremely well. He could stop worrying about his fall and continue preparing for his big test.

No amount of last-minute cramming, however, could make up for the work Stephen had skipped in the last three years. The night before the exam he could hardly sleep. Dutifully, he dressed in the uniform required of all exam candidates—black robes, white shirt, and a bow tie. During the test, he carefully selected the questions he could answer best.

Afterward, Stephen celebrated gleefully with his friends. But his fatigue must have affected his test performance. When the results were announced, he was on the border between a First and a Second. The test examiners called him in for an interview to decide which degree to award.

Stephen's doubts had vanished. He felt confident again and ready for a little humor. "If I get a First, I shall go to Cambridge," he told his examiners. "If I receive a Second, I will remain at Oxford. So I expect that you will give me a First."

A tower guards the northern end of King's Parade at Caius College. Caius is a part of Cambridge University, one of the oldest universities in the world.

COSMOLOGY

Stephen was right. After spending the summer traveling, he went off to Cambridge University. Two paths were open to him. He could study particle physics or cosmology. Particle physics deals with the very small. This area of physics covers atomic and subatomic particles that are almost too tiny to be imagined. Cosmology deals with the huge. It covers the history of the entire universe, or cosmos. Cosmology asks the ambitious question: where does the universe come from?

Stephen decided to pursue cosmology. He hoped to do research under world-famous cosmologist Fred Hoyle. Instead, he was assigned to a lesser-known scientist, Dennis Sciama. At first, it seemed like a setback to his goals. But Sciama proved to be an excellent scientist and an inspiring supervisor. He was always ready to discuss Stephen's ideas.

To understand cosmology, Stephen had to study some complicated mathematical equations that had been developed by the late scientist Albert Einstein. They were called the theory of general relativity. Einstein's work had dramatically changed the way scientists looked at gravity. Gravity is what holds everything onto Earth instead of it all flying off into space. Before Einstein, most people had held to the theories of the great British scientist Sir Isaac Newton. Newton described gravity as a force of attraction between two bodies. When you toss a ball into the air, gravity will make it come right back down.

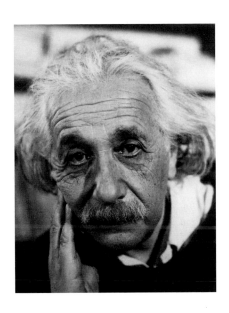

Albert Einstein (right) *changed the way scientists think about physics.*

But according to Einstein, gravity isn't a force. Einstein said that physical objects bend the space around them. Even stranger, Einstein said that space and time are so closely related that they comprise a single entity—space-time. Objects actually bend the space-time around them. That's what gravity is—curves in space-time. For a small object like a tennis ball, the curve is incredibly small. But for a large object like the sun, the curve is big enough to measure. It's the curves in space-time that make a ball fall back to the ground again or keep a planet circling the Sun instead of flying off into outer space.

Even for someone as brilliant as Stephen, following Einstein's mathematical equations was rough going.

Stephen had not taken a great deal of math as an undergraduate, and he was not used to working very hard at his studies. When he also had a hard time choosing a research topic, Sciama began to wonder if Stephen could successfully complete the program.

GENERAL RELATIVITY AND GRAVITY

Scientists have a model to help us understand how physical objects can bend the empty space around them. Imagine a tightly stretched elastic sheet, like the surface of a trampoline. As long as nothing rests on the sheet, it remains smooth and flat. If someone puts a heavy item, like a bowling ball, on the trampoline, it sags. The bowling ball lies at the bottom of its own small valley. Things get interesting when a smaller ball is also placed on the trampoline and set in motion. If the small ball travels at exactly the right speed, it can be made to circle around and around the bowling ball. It will follow the outline of the valley made by the bowling ball.

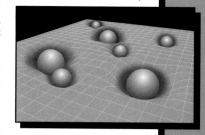

Of course, this two-dimensional example is greatly simplified. But scientists say something very similar happens in three-dimensional space. An enormous object like the Sun curves the space-time surrounding it. This traps any nearby planets into circular orbits around the Sun. The

An artist's two-dimensional illustration of gravity

reason the planets don't fall into the Sun is that they are traveling too fast. If the planets slowed down or stopped, they would slide down the curvature of space and collide with the Sun.

SOMETHING WRONG

Besides his studies, another concern gnawed at Stephen. He was getting clumsier. Simple things, like tying his shoelaces, were suddenly becoming more difficult. Talking was harder too. Sometimes he struggled to get out his words. Sciama thought he had a slight speech impediment. But it did not seem serious, and Stephen forced himself to focus on other things.

During Christmas vacation, however, his parents were struck by the change in Stephen's speech. It was an extremely cold winter, and the lake at Saint Albans had frozen solid. One day Stephen's mother suggested that he go ice-skating. It's not unusual for an amateur skater to take a tumble, but when Stephen fell, he could scarcely get up again. His arms and legs weren't doing what they were supposed to do. Isobel Hawking knew at once that something was terribly wrong. She took her son to the local doctor who advised that Stephen have further medical tests.

In the middle of this anxious time, Stephen attended a New Year's Eve party to welcome in 1963. One of the guests was a girl named Jane Wilde, who was several years younger than Stephen. The two struck up a friendly conversation. When Stephen told Jane he was studying cosmology, she had no idea what that was. But she was strongly drawn to the brilliant and charming young man. She sensed both his pride and his utter bewilderment at what was happening to his body. Stephen liked Jane too. He invited her to his twenty-first birthday party several days later. A large collection of Stephen's relatives and school friends crowded into the Hawking home to celebrate.

Several days after his birthday, Stephen entered the hospital. Doctors administered test after test while Stephen lay in bed helpless and mystified. Despite his anxiety, he knew his situation could be worse. In the bed across from him, a boy died of leukemia. By comparison, Stephen could be grateful that he was alive and not in pain.

The medical tests lasted about two weeks. Stephen, who wanted to know everything about the cosmos, asked very little about himself. He could tell the doctors didn't have good news, and he hadn't the heart to ask for details. All he knew was that his case was unusual, he would probably get worse, and there was nothing the doctors could do but prescribe vitamins. Their best advice was that Stephen should keep working on his Ph.D.

Stephen returned to Cambridge. But he saw little point in continuing his studies. Deeply depressed, he spent a good deal of time listening to the gloomy music of German composer Richard Wagner. Stephen had a disease called amyotrophic lateral sclerosis, or ALS. In Great Britain, it is usually called motor neuron disease because the nerves that control muscle movement stop working properly. Americans usually refer to it as Lou Gehrig's disease, after a famous baseball player who died of the illness. Over a period of time, Stephen's muscles would become paralyzed and waste away. There was no known way to stop it. The doctors told him that he had about two years to live.

Stephen's whole world had come crashing down, and he didn't know what to do. "How could something like this happen to me?" he wondered. "Why should I be cut off like this?" But whenever he felt too sorry for himself, he remembered the boy who had died.

A NEW OUTLOOK

Jane already knew of Stephen's condition when, one day, she accidentally met him at the train station.

Stephen and Lou Gehrig (right) are two of the most famous cases of ALS. But around 350,000 people throughout the world are suffering from the disease.

Except that he looked neater and his hair was cut shorter, she thought Stephen seemed much the same. And despite the tumult of his emotions, he smiled as broadly as if he hadn't a care in the world. The two sat together as they rode into London. Afterward, Stephen asked Jane to the opera and six weeks later to the May Ball in Cambridge. By then Stephen's condition had begun to worsen noticeably. Jane wasn't even sure he had the strength to drive his father's old car to the festivities. Stephen not only drove, he sped furiously through the countryside. Jane was terrified, but Stephen got her safely to the ball and back.

As the doctors had predicted, Stephen's condition was going downhill. When Jane met Stephen again that November, he was very unsteady on his feet. But he was also stubbornly energetic, and he refused to talk about his illness. One time Jane asked about a recent trip to see a doctor. "He told me not to come back because there's nothing he can do," Stephen replied.

The couple continued to meet and attend operas. When he was with Jane, Stephen felt as if he had a future after all. Although he could still be depressed and he detested using a walking stick, Stephen's illness forced him to change his outlook. Prior to his illness, he had been a bored young man. Facing death, he realized how precious life is. One night he dreamed that he was going to be executed. If only he were spared, what wonderful and important things he could do! Several times he also dreamed that he would give up his own life in order to save others. Hope and a sense of possibility stirred within Stephen. He began to take his work more seriously. "I found to my surprise," he recalled, "that I was enjoying life in the present more than I had before." Then, to his great joy, Jane agreed to become his wife. Stephen Hawking had found a reason to look forward.

Sir Fred Hoyle was a world-famous cosmologist. He taught and researched at Cambridge while Stephen was earning his Ph.D.

Chapter **THREE**

HAPPIER THAN BEFORE

STEPHEN HAD TAKEN ON A BIG RESPONSIBILITY. To support himself and Jane, he had to have a job. That meant he would have to complete his Ph.D. To receive his degree, Stephen would have to do original research on an important topic and write a doctoral thesis. But he still didn't know what to write about.

Even though Stephen wasn't studying under Fred Hoyle, he was in touch with Hoyle's graduate students, including Jayant Narlikar. Narlikar shared with Stephen some difficult mathematical equations that he and Hoyle were trying to solve. Later, Stephen attended a meeting of the Royal Society, an important scientific organization. He listened to Hoyle present views based on those equations. Hoyle believed that the universe had always existed and always would. This idea is called the steady state theory.

After Hoyle's speech, Stephen rose slowly and told the famous cosmologist that there was a mistake in his calculations. "How do you know?" asked Hoyle.

"Because I worked it out," replied Stephen. Hoyle was embarrassed and angry. Other scientists in the audience remembered the outspoken physics student.

Stephen still needed to find a thesis topic. Sciama knew that a lively exchange of ideas can stimulate creativity. His students began attending a series of physics lectures being held in London. Soon they became interested in the work of a mathematician named Roger Penrose. Penrose was studying what happens to stars that collapse after they run out of fuel to keep them burning.

According to Penrose, a dying star could collapse all the way down to a singularity—a point with no dimensions. It is also a place where the laws of physics break down. What held true for the rest of the universe would not necessarily hold true for singularities. The idea intrigued Stephen. How could an enormous star shrink to the very limit of existence? Would the laws of physics really break down? Stephen became eager to discover all he could about singularities.

COLLAPSING STARS

Roger Penrose built his theory of singularities on Einstein's theory of general relativity. As early as 1919, scientists had proved Einstein's claim that massive bodies like the Sun curve space-time around them. The denser the object, the more space-time curves. For example, a ball made of foam rubber is not as dense as a smaller ball of solid iron. The smaller ball has more substance to it, or matter. That means it also has greater gravity. It curves space to a greater degree.

All stars produce heat and light during a process called nuclear fusion. During nuclear fusion, the nuclei of the atoms of the element hydrogen fuse together to form another element, helium. After billions of years, the hydrogen is all used up. The star begins to collapse inward under the pressure of its own gravity. The matter in the star is squeezed together. Although the star becomes smaller in size, its density increases. This makes the star's gravity greater also. It distorts space even more than it did previously.

Sometimes the star becomes a white dwarf, a star with a radius of only a few thousand miles. Hundreds of tons of matter are packed within each cubic inch of a white dwarf. Einstein's theory predicted that certain stars would collapse even further. Such stars, only about 10 miles (16 kilometers) in diameter would contain millions of tons of matter for each cubic inch. Although astronomers had shown that white dwarves exist, no one had ever discovered these much denser stars.

But under certain conditions, a burned-out star could keep on collapsing to an infinitely small point—at least in theory. This was the singularity that Penrose was talking about. Billions and billions of tons of matter would have been pressed into an area smaller than an atom.

In the early 1960s, when Stephen was a graduate student, scientists didn't know if singularities were real. All they could say was that according to Einstein's theory, singularities *should* exist.

AN EXPANDING UNIVERSE

One evening Stephen was staring out a train window on his way home from another lecture in London. He imagined an enormous sun shrinking down to a singularity, and an amazing thought came to him. What would happen if the whole process were reversed? What if a singularity, infinitely small but infinitely dense, were suddenly to explode? Could that explain how the universe came into existence?

The idea that the vast universe had erupted from something smaller than the smallest atomic particle was astounding but hardly new. In 1922 a Russian mathematician named Alexander Friedmann suggested that the universe was expanding. According to Friedmann's calculations, the distances between stars were increasing as the universe got bigger. But no astronomer had measured or observed this expansion.

In 1927 a Belgian priest and astronomer, Georges-Henri Lemaître, proposed a daring idea. He believed that the entire universe had once been condensed into what he called the cosmic egg, or primordial atom. From this incredibly small beginning, matter and energy had spread out to form the stars, galaxies, and planets. This idea would develop into the big bang theory.

Meanwhile, astronomers were building bigger and better telescopes. They were able to study all kinds of information about the stars. Just two years after Lemaître announced his theory of the cosmic egg, an astronomer named Edwin Hubble used the enormous telescope at the Mount Wilson Observatory in California to show that the universe is really expanding. Scientists had experimental proof.

Some scientists didn't like the idea of the universe having a beginning. It bothered them that the laws of physics could say nothing about what came before that beginning. Like Fred Hoyle, these scientists found it easier to believe in the steady state theory. It said that the universe had always existed. Stephen believed this as a teenager. But Lemaître's cosmic egg seemed very much like the singularity of some collapsed stars. If a star could shrink to form a singularity, perhaps a singularity could explode the way Lemaître suggested. Stephen told his supervisor that he wanted to apply Roger Penrose's work on singularities to the whole universe. He thought he might come up with mathematical evidence for the big bang.

Although Dennis Sciama believed in the steady state theory, he knew an interesting idea when he heard one. "Yes. Good. Do that," he told Stephen.

THE COLOR OF STARLIGHT

Scientists figured out that the universe is expanding by studying the color of light given off by distant stars. White light can be broken up into different colors by passing through a prism. We refer to these colors— red, orange, yellow, green, blue, indigo, and violet— as the visible spectrum. The different colors of light correspond to different wavelengths of energy.

One way to think of light waves is to imagine them as waves rippling across a pond. Wavelength is the distance from the crest (top) of one wave to the crest of the next. Red light has the longest wavelength; blue light has the shortest.

Astronomers observed that light from distant stars is shifted slightly toward the longer wavelengths. This makes sense if the universe is getting bigger. As the stars move away from us, their wavelengths are stretched out, and their colors are shifted toward the red end of the spectrum. Scientists say they are redshifted. If the universe were contracting, wavelengths would be compressed as the stars moved closer and closer together. This would shift

Never in his entire life had Stephen worked so hard. "To my surprise, I liked it," he wrote later. "Maybe it is not fair to call it work." In his doctoral thesis of 1965, Stephen used mathematics to show that the universe began in a big bang. His paper made many cosmologists reconsider their ideas on the origin of the universe.

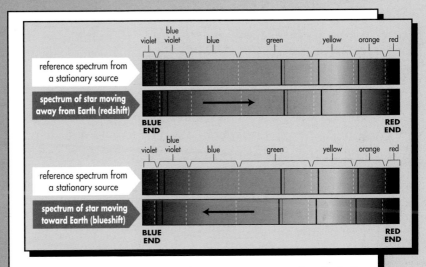

If a star's spectrum shows red lines, the star is moving away from Earth. If a star's spectrum shows blue lines, it is moving toward Earth.

their colors toward the blue end of the spectrum. This phenomenon is known as the Doppler effect, after the nineteenth-century scientist Christian Doppler, who discovered it.

YOUNG RESEARCHER

With his Ph.D. nearly complete, Stephen could apply for a paid research fellowship, a grant to do research in his field. Stephen's disease was still advancing. He could no longer grip a pen easily or strike the keys on a typewriter. He was counting on Jane, who was still attending college in London, to type his fellowship application form for him. When Jane arrived that weekend with a broken arm, he thought she wouldn't be able to help him after all. But it was Jane's left arm that was broken, and she was right-handed. She copied down the answers Stephen dictated, then a friend typed the application.

Soon Stephen received a fellowship at Caius (pronounced Keys) College in Cambridge. Nothing more stood in the way of his future with Jane. In July 1965, Stephen and Jane were married. Holding a cane but standing straight and tall, Stephen posed for wedding pictures with his bride. He had already surpassed the doctors' predictions. No one knew how much longer he might live. But Stephen and Jane were filled with hope and love and courage as they began their life together. They certainly weren't going to allow Stephen's disability to hold them back.

On their return to Cambridge, the newlyweds settled in a house on Little Saint Mary's Lane. The Hawkings loved to have friends over for lunch or dinner. While music played in the background, the guests cheerfully helped with the cooking. Then they crowded around the dining table, trying to stick to general topics but sometimes discussing physics in spite of themselves. There was nothing Stephen liked better. Singularities still fascinated him. Teamed up with Roger Penrose, he continued to investigate these baffling phenomena.

Stephen's research was causing ripples of interest among other physicists. At Christmastime he was invited to give a speech at a relativity meeting in Miami,

Florida. Eagerly, Stephen and Jane set off for the United States. They enjoyed the view from their beachfront hotel and accepted an invitation to visit Texas.

Stephen and Jane had both needed a vacation because they were intensely busy in England. Jane stayed in London during the week, still working on her college degree. On Fridays she hurried to Cambridge to spend time with Stephen. It was getting even more difficult for Stephen to move around. He had to exchange his walking sticks for crutches. Going upstairs to his bedroom might take him as long as fifteen minutes. But he refused to give in to his disease. He would rather do things slowly than accept help. John Boslough, who wrote a book about Hawking, called him "the toughest man I know."

Stephen was also tough when it came to his work. At Cambridge he met some of the top scientists in the world. He wasn't afraid to ask them challenging questions. Some people thought Stephen was brash, but he was also sensitive and full of humor. His sheer intellect was daunting, but he was lots of fun.

"I was happier than I'd been before," Stephen said of this fulfilling time. In 1967, four years after he was diagnosed with ALS, Stephen's first child, Robert, was born. Stephen was pleased to be a father and determined to provide a good life for his newborn son. A promising future, both personally and professionally, stretched before him.

Arno Penzias (left) *and Robert Wilson stand on the radio antenna with which they discovered microwaves in outer space.*

Chapter **FOUR**

THE RIDDLE OF BLACK HOLES

WHILE STEPHEN AND PENROSE WERE STUDYING singularities, scientists had been making some exciting discoveries. In 1965 two researchers, Arno Penzias and Robert Wilson, had detected faint microwaves, part of the range of electromagnetic waves, in outer space. Usually scientists could locate the source of such radiation. But these microwaves did not come from a particular area. They seemed to be spread evenly throughout the universe. For a time, the researchers were mystified. Finally, their investigation revealed that the microwaves were likely background radiation left over from the explosion, the big bang, at the beginning of the universe.

Two years later, another major finding rocked the world of astronomy. A postgraduate student at Cambridge, Jocelyn Bell, discovered regularly spaced pulses of radiation coming from outer space. Because they were at the low energy end of the spectrum, scientists classified them as radio waves. The pattern of these pulses, or radio waves, was so exact that some scientists wondered if they came from an alien civilization. More and more of the strange pulses were discovered, and it became obvious that they couldn't all be from extraterrestrials or outer space life. Soon scientists realized that the pulses were coming from partially collapsed stars. They called the stars pulsars. The signals appeared so regularly because the stars were rotating on their axis. Their beams of radio noise sweep past Earth the way the rotating beacon in a lighthouse sweeps past ships at sea.

Black Holes

The matter in pulsars (also called neutron stars) has been compressed so tightly that even a cupful would weigh tons. Perhaps other stars could collapse even further. Even if a star did not shrink down all the way to a singularity, it could become incredibly dense. The denser it became, the stronger its gravity would be. A star's gravity might become so strong that even light could not escape its tug. It still would not be a singularity. But since no light from such a star could reach our eyes, it would be invisible to us.

THE ELECTROMAGNETIC SPECTRUM

Visible light isn't the only form of electromagnetic radiation. Some forms of electromagnetic radiation have wavelengths that are much longer or shorter than the light we see with our eyes. Radio waves have the longest wavelengths. They also have very low energy. At the opposite end of the spectrum, gamma rays have the shortest wavelengths. From the longest to the shortest, electromagnetic radiation is classified as follows:

Radio waves
Microwaves
Infrared radiation
Visible light
Ultraviolet radiation
X-rays
Gamma radiation

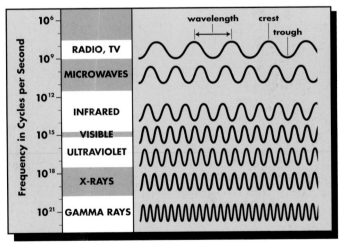

The small numbers to the right of the 10 indicate the number of zeros after the one.

Newspaper stories about gravitationally collapsed stars began to appear. The public was fascinated. In 1969 a noted cosmologist, John Wheeler, was giving a talk at a physics meeting in New York. He got tired of saying "gravitationally collapsed stars" over and over. A new term occurred to him—black holes. The popular press took up the name. Suddenly it seemed that everyone was talking and writing about black holes.

Stephen liked the new name. It was catchy and clever. If the big bang theory was correct, the universe had begun as a singularity. Was it possible that, under certain conditions, a star could end as a singularity? It seemed to Stephen as if the whole universe was like a

Roger Penrose (above) **worked with Stephen. They studied the mysteries of the universe.**

giant black hole turned inside out. He continued to investigate what this meant with Roger Penrose. Finally, in 1970, they published the results of their work. In his Ph.D. thesis, Stephen had shown that the universe had exploded into existence in the big bang. With Penrose he developed the idea further, proving that this was the only way the universe could have begun. According to Einstein's theory of general relativity, there was no other possibility.

"The biggest misunderstanding about the big bang," Stephen once explained, "is that it began as a lump of matter somewhere in the void of space. It was not just matter that was created during the big bang. It was space and time that were created." Most people find it hard to imagine a nothingness without time or space.

A Puzzling Contradiction
Stephen and Penrose had produced a stunning piece of work. Other scientists were beginning to take note of Stephen. But something still bothered him. General relativity wasn't the whole story. There was also quantum mechanics, or particle physics—the study of the behavior of particles smaller than atoms. The problem is that general relativity and quantum physics don't work together. Both theories make sense; both work. But both could not be true. Scientists all over the world were stumped.

One reason for the dilemma is that in general relativity, all events have a cause and effect. Everything happens for a reason. With enough knowledge, scientists can predict what will happen in a given set of circumstances. General relativity works just fine for things on a large scale. For example, it can predict the orbits of planets or the degree to which light traveling through space is bent when it passes by a star.

When it comes to events at the atomic or quantum level, general relativity is no use at all. At first, scientists thought they should be able to predict the way an elementary particle, such as a proton or electron, moved. But what worked for stars and planets did not work for particles.

Scientists simply could not pin the particles down. If they knew how fast a particle was moving, they could never be sure of its position in space. If they knew its position, they could never be sure of its speed. This phenomenon is called the uncertainty principle. According to general relativity, scientists should be able to predict anything. But according to quantum physics, there is a limit to what scientists can predict. Stephen and Penrose's proof of the big bang was based solely on general relativity. It took no account of quantum mechanics.

By this time, Stephen had been asked to join the Institute of Theoretical Astronomy in Cambridge. As his reputation grew, important astronomers and physicists from all over the world wanted to talk with him. Three times a week, Stephen drove to the institute in a three-wheeled car especially made for the disabled. After resisting as long as he could, he had traded in his crutches for a wheelchair. But he refused to see this as a sign of defeat. "Stephen doesn't make any concessions to his illness," Jane once explained, "and I don't make any concessions to him." At the institute, Stephen pushed himself as hard as he could. He expected other people to do the same.

EVENT HORIZON AND ENTROPHY

In 1970 Stephen's second child Lucy was born. One night, when his daughter was a newborn, Stephen was thinking about black holes. In his past work, he had concentrated on the heart of a black hole. He began instead to focus on its boundary: where did a black hole begin, and where did it end?

The distance at which light can no longer escape the gravity of a black hole is called its event horizon. A sudden insight came to Stephen as he slowly got into bed. He realized that the event horizon, or edge, of a black hole can never get any smaller. Things fall into a black hole, and nothing can leave. Obviously, it couldn't shrink. But Stephen saw way beyond the obvious. He was so excited that he couldn't sleep that night.

After Stephen's inspiration came lots of hard work. He wanted to understand everything about black holes. So did other physicists. A graduate student in physics at Princeton University, Jacob Bekenstein, disagreed with some of Stephen's ideas. Bekenstein said that the size of the event horizon around a black hole had entropy. Entropy is the measure of disorder in a system. As a system breaks down into disorder, it can't be returned to order. If Bekenstein was right and there was disorder in black holes, that would mean that black holes were breaking down.

At first, Stephen thought this was absolute nonsense. In order for a system to have entropy, it had to have a temperature. It had to radiate energy. A black hole cannot possibly radiate energy, Stephen said, because nothing could escape from a black hole. But some other physicists weren't so sure.

In September 1973, Stephen visited Moscow, Russia. Two Russian physicists, Yakov Zeldovich and Alexander Starobinsky, explained why they thought black holes could create and emit particles. Stephen thought about it carefully. Was it possible that black holes sent radiation into space? Zeldovich and Starobinsky's arguments sounded quite possible to Stephen. But he questioned their mathematics.

After his trip, Stephen began working on the problem himself. Creative instinct plays a strong role in his thinking process. "I work very much on intuition," he has said, "thinking that, well, a certain idea ought to be right. Then I try to prove it. Sometimes I find I'm wrong. Sometimes I find that the original idea was wrong, but that leads to a new idea." Stephen's argument with Bekenstein was beginning to take him in a new direction. He decided to take another look at the uncertainty principle.

WHY BLACK HOLES AREN'T BLACK

According to the uncertainty principle, our information about the universe can never be complete. Although this sounds simple, it leads to some strange ideas. Stephen knew that what we think of as the vacuum, or emptiness of space, isn't really empty at all. If it were, that would be a kind of absolute knowledge, and the uncertainty principle doesn't allow absolute knowledge.

Quantum physicists believe that there may be pairs of particles (much smaller than an atom) popping in and out of existence all the time. But the physicists cannot determine whether these particles have enough energy to really exist. They say that the particles exist on "borrowed" energy. That makes them "virtual" particles. They are not considered "real."

Usually one member of a pair of virtual particles has a positive charge and one has a negative charge. Since positive and negative charges cannot exist together, the two cancel each other out. The virtual particles are destroyed so quickly that they have hardly existed at all.

But Stephen's scientific intuition told him that something different can happen near a black hole. The negative particle (which lacks the energy to get away) is likely to be sucked into the black hole before it has a chance to interact with its positive counterpart. This means that the positive particle is not destroyed and escapes into space. It is no longer a virtual particle. It is a real particle. Such escaping particles could be considered as radiation from the black hole. Perhaps black holes aren't as black as scientists believed.

CAN BLACK HOLES DISAPPEAR?

It seemed as if Stephen's creativity had gone into overdrive as he grappled with these new ideas and equations. Because he can't write down his equations, he has to hold them all in his head. Although he has a strong memory and carefully works out the equations for his theories, it's difficult to keep track of so many numbers in his mind. Instead, he tends to think in pictures. Stephen had built up a very interesting picture of black holes. They are areas of almost unimaginable density. Their gravity is so great that not even light can escape from the surface of a black hole. Yet, against all expectations, black holes radiate particles into space.

Stephen had something else amazing to add to this picture. His reasoning was simple. The virtual particles that fall into a black hole change it. Since many of them have a negative charge, they can't add anything to the hole. Instead, they take something away. The black hole loses energy and mass because of them. A kind of cycle is set up. The tremendous gravity around a black hole causes more virtual particles to be formed than in other areas of space. That means that there are plenty of negative particles to fall into the hole. As more and more of the negative particles enter the black hole, the hole loses more and more mass and energy. At the same time, it becomes hotter and begins to radiate even more rapidly.

Could the black hole's mass ever vanish completely? Nobody knows for certain, but Stephen believes that it can. When a black hole reaches a certain temperature and a certain rate of radiation, it will explode. This will happen while it still has a mass about the size of an asteroid—18 miles (30 km) or more in diameter. If Stephen is correct, the whole mass will explode at once with the force of millions of hydrogen bombs. But it would take billions and billions of years for a black hole to lose all its mass and explode. To get an idea of the time frame, write one followed by sixty-six zeroes. That's longer than the life span of the entire universe!

STEPHEN'S CHANGED EVERYTHING!

Stephen knew that other people would have a hard time accepting his ideas. In fact, Stephen too was amazed by the idea of black holes emitting radiation. He had come a long way from his bedtime insight when Lucy was a baby. Then he had said that the event horizon of a black hole could never get smaller. Now he was saying that black holes could disappear entirely.

Lucy was three years old, and Stephen was still struggling with the problem. Christmas vacation of 1973 found him more preoccupied with black holes than ever. Over and over, he replayed the equations in his head. He couldn't stop checking himself.

By early January, Stephen was ready to share his work with Dennis Sciama. He feared his old adviser might be skeptical. But Sciama was enthusiastic. Stephen's ideas were bold and original. His mathematics was sound. Sciama said he would like to tell some of his colleagues what Stephen was doing. Stephen agreed.

The news traveled fast. On Stephen's thirty-second birthday, he was interrupted by a phone call in the middle of dinner. A fascinated Roger Penrose wanted to hear about Stephen's work. Forgetting all about time, Stephen plunged into the discussion. By the time he returned to the table, forty-five minutes had passed and his special birthday dinner was cold.

Stephen began to tell a few others about his work. A scientist named Martin Rees became very excited by their talk. "Have you heard?" he asked, when he ran into Dennis Sciama. "Stephen's changed everything!"

Despite such support, Stephen must have been nervous when he officially presented his findings at a conference the next month. He tried to soften the impact a little by placing a question mark after the title of his talk. "Black Hole Explosions?" read the subject of his speech. Using diagrams that were projected onto the wall, he presented his theory that black holes emit radiation. He explained that the holes eventually disappear in an explosion.

Strong Reaction

Stephen's colleagues had become used to his slurred speech. They listened carefully to catch each word. But when Stephen was done, they were too stunned to comment or ask questions. What Stephen suggested seemed bizarre beyond imagination.

Finally, the chairman of the conference, physicist John G. Taylor, jumped up and cried, "Sorry, Stephen, but this is absolute rubbish." He yanked another scientist from his seat. Then stalked out. Stephen could only watch in amazement and dismay.

One month later, on March 1, 1974, Stephen published his paper in an important scientific journal, *Nature*. Soon physicists all over the world were talking about it. Some scientists were skeptical of the new theory. Others were excited and impressed. They checked and rechecked Stephen's calculations and concluded that he was right.

"In the end," Stephen noted years later, "even the chairman agreed that I was right." Sciama proudly called Stephen's paper "one of the most beautiful in the history of physics."

The particles that were supposed to escape from black holes soon became known as "Hawking radiation." But as convincing as Stephen's mathematical proofs were, no one knew for sure if black holes really existed. It would be up to astronomers to find out.

Stephen spent a year at the California Institute of Technology.

Chapter **FIVE**

AN END TO PHYSICS?

STEPHEN'S REPUTATION SOARED. **O**NLY SEVERAL WEEKS after his talk on black holes, a famous scientific organization, the Royal Society, invited Stephen to become a member. At thirty-two, he was one of the youngest people ever to receive this honor. During the induction ceremony in London, Stephen couldn't walk onstage with the other new members. The president of the society carried the membership book down to his seat. With great difficulty, Stephen signed his name in the book. The audience broke into applause.

Soon another invitation set the whole Hawking family packing. Stephen was asked to spend a year at the California Institute of Technology, Caltech, the famous science university in Pasadena. Jane, four-year-old

Lucy, and seven-year-old Robert loved the sunny, warm climate. The children visited Disneyland with their mother, and sometimes their father joined them for short trips up and down the coast.

DISCOVERY OF A BLACK HOLE?

Stephen made good friends at Caltech. He enjoyed working with noted cosmologist Kip Thorne. Sometimes the two discussed the progress astronomers were making on locating a black hole. Both men were eager for physical proof that black holes really existed. Several years earlier, astronomers had discovered a star in the constellation Cygnus that might have an invisible companion orbiting it. When two stars orbit each other, they are said to be a binary system. Scientists

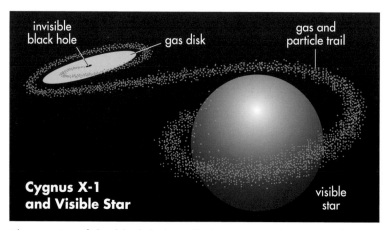

The gravity of the black hole pulls in gases and particles from its companion star.

thought that the visible star (called HDE226868) might be part of a binary system because it seemed to be reacting to a strong gravitational field. But there was nothing nearby to create such a field. Astronomers guessed that a black hole might be the cause of the star's strange behavior. They dubbed this possible black hole Cygnus X-1. Stephen and Kip Thorne were very excited by the news.

AT HOME IN ENGLAND

When the Hawkings returned to England in 1975, they were ready to make some changes. The family moved into a large, first-floor apartment. Stephen would not have to climb stairs. The doorways were wide enough for a wheelchair to pass through. But Stephen needed even more help than the new apartment could give. He had to struggle to get in and out of bed. Lifting food from his plate to his mouth became very difficult. Jane didn't have enough time to look after Stephen and her children.

Since the Hawkings could not afford a nurse to take care of Stephen, they asked one of Stephen's research students to move into the apartment with them. The student, who received free room and board, would help Stephen with dressing, eating, bathing, and getting to and from work. It was considered an honor to live with the Hawkings. One live-in student said it was "like participating in history."

Stephen's condition had worsened so much that he

could no longer use his special car. It was replaced with an electric wheelchair. Stephen drove his wheelchair hard and fast. As he rolled carelessly into the streets, he counted on the approaching cars and his assistants to look out for him. He also developed a habit of running his wheelchair lightly over people's toes when they displeased him. At home Stephen spun rapidly around the garden as he played tag with his children. He only wished that he could play more physical games with them. Jane was the one to teach Robert and Lucy to play cricket (a ball game similar to baseball), crowing happily, "I can get them out!"

Despite their hectic schedules, Stephen and Jane found time to share many pastimes. They enjoyed going to concerts and plays. The local theater had a special seat that could be removed when they received word that Stephen was coming for a performance. He could drive right in and park his wheelchair in the empty space. The Hawkings also continued to host dinner parties. Sometimes as many as sixty guests crammed into the apartment. But although Jane felt great satisfaction as a wife and mother, she wanted something more in her life. The new living arrangements in the Hawking household allowed her to return to school. She began working toward a Ph.D. in medieval languages.

AN ANSWER FOR EINSTEIN

In 1975 and 1976, Stephen won six major awards, including a medal given by the science academy at the Vatican, the center of the Roman Catholic Church. "The joy and excitement of Stephen's success were tremendous," Jane recalled. He began to accept more speaking engagements and visited the United States again in the winter of 1976. In some ways, it was a difficult trip. Often when he arrived to speak in an auditorium, there was no handicapped access to the stage. Friends and fellow scientists had to lift him up to it in his heavy wheelchair. Stephen didn't enjoy arriving in this way, but he had a sense of mischief. Sometimes, when he was introduced, he zoomed forward in his chair at top speed. People gasped in horror, certain he would fall off the stage. But Stephen managed to stop at the very edge. Although he lightened his lectures with jokes, his speech had become so slurred that it was difficult to understand. Many people had to rely on others to interpret what he had said.

At the end of one speech in Boston, Stephen reminded the audience of one of Albert Einstein's favorite sayings: "God doesn't play dice." Einstein had used these words to oppose the uncertainty principle. According to this principle, we cannot determine the cause of everything that happens in the universe. Even as more and more scientists came to believe in the uncertainty principle, Einstein refused to accept it. There had to be a reason for everything that happened. And if there was, sooner or later scientists would discover it.

On the other hand, Stephen was firmly convinced of the uncertainty principle. His theory of black holes was based upon it. Stephen had an answer for Albert Einstein. "God not only plays dice," Stephen declared, "he sometimes throws them where they can't be seen." Like Einstein, Stephen believed that someday a great theory of physics would be discovered. But he did not believe that theory would do away with uncertainty. A certain amount of uncertainty is built into the very fabric of the universe.

Stephen's U.S. lectures brought him lots of publicity, but he was becoming a hit in Great Britain too. The British Broadcasting Company (BBC) made a special documentary on Stephen, *The Key to the Universe*. Millions of British people tuned in to watch it. Officials at Cambridge felt it was time to give Stephen more responsibility. They created a special position in gravitational physics for him in 1977. They also made him a full professor at Caius College. One year later, Stephen received another important honor—the Albert Einstein Award, which was announced in Washington, D.C.

THE END OF PHYSICS?

The year 1979 was especially busy and joyful for Stephen. He published a book to commemorate Einstein's one-hundredth birthday on March 14, 1979. That same month, Jane gave birth to their third child, a little boy named Timothy. And one month after that, Stephen became the Lucasian professor at Cambridge's

Department of Applied Mathematics and Theoretical Physics (DAMTP). About 310 years earlier, Sir Isaac Newton, who developed classical physics, had also been the Lucasian professor. A special ceremony was held to welcome Stephen to his new position. One of his students read aloud the lecture Stephen had prepared for the event.

"Is the End in Sight for Theoretical Physics?" asked the title of Stephen's talk. Ever optimistic, Stephen hoped that a theory of everything would be found before the end of the twentieth century. That left scientists only twenty-one years to tie everything together, but Stephen thought computers could help. Noting their rapid development, he imagined a time when computers wouldn't need humans to tell them what to do. Intelligent machines might even do physics on their own. "So maybe," Stephen concluded with offbeat humor, "the end is in sight for theoretical physicists, if not for theoretical physics."

Stephen's new university position meant a great deal to him. Several months later, he realized he hadn't signed the historic record of Lucasian professors. Although he had little control over the muscles in his hand, he insisted on doing so. Gripping the pen awkwardly, he managed to slowly form the letters. It was the last time he signed his name.

Stephen works in his office at Cambridge University.

Chapter **SIX**

BOUNDARIES TO THE UNIVERSE?

As LUCASIAN PROFESSOR, STEPHEN RATED HIS OWN office at the DAMTP. He liked to give visitors a chuckle as soon as they arrived at his door. "Quiet Please, The Boss Is Asleep," read his new sign. The sign in his old quarters had read "Black Holes Are Out of Sight." Bookshelves and a large desk with family photos took up most of the space in Stephen's new office. He had a special telephone that allowed him to talk without holding the receiver. An automatic page-turner let him flip through a book by simply touching a button. And special levers on his computer helped him record his ideas without using a keyboard.

Although Stephen spent almost two hours getting ready for work, he was usually in his office by 10:00 A.M.

Morning coffee and afternoon tea gave him a chance to mingle with colleagues and students. One of his assistants held Stephen's cup so he could drink. He spoke little, but everyone stopped to listen when Stephen had something to say. Sometimes the discussions grew animated. Students scribbled especially good insights onto one of the tabletops in the common room. "When we want to save something," said Stephen, "we just xerox the table." Generally Stephen remained at work until about 7:00 P.M.

RIGHTS FOR DISABLED PEOPLE

As busy as he was, Stephen still made time to fight for the rights of disabled individuals. He sent forceful letters to the Cambridge City Council demanding ramps in public buildings and lowered curbs in busy areas. After one election, Stephen told the council that polling places had to be made more accessible to the disabled. When he had gone to vote, he had a terrible time getting into the building. The local press began highlighting the issue. Stephen got the improvements he demanded.

"It is no use complaining about the public's attitude about the disabled," Stephen has said. "It is up to disabled people to change people's awareness in the same way that blacks and women have changed public perceptions." Stephen has also become outspoken about environmental issues and the need to help the poor.

THE NO BOUNDARY PROPOSAL

Physics continued to be the most exciting thing in Stephen's life. He was working on a new theory that had to do with the beginning of the universe. Although Stephen had already proved that the universe began with a big bang, he was beginning to reconsider some of his ideas. According to his previous way of thinking, the big bang created time, space, and the laws of physics. Nothing could be known about reality prior to the moment of creation. This bothered Stephen. If the laws of physics did not apply *before* the big bang, might there be other times and places in the universe where they didn't apply? Stephen didn't like this idea any more than Einstein had liked the uncertainty principle.

Could quantum mechanics make a difference? Stephen began to apply the principles of quantum physics to the big bang as he had already done with black holes. Once again, the mathematics he used led to some amazing conclusions. As scientists look backward in time toward the big bang, matter becomes so dense that the strength of gravity is unbelievable. Space is so warped by the gravity that space curls around on itself. Time is affected too. Time is bent around so tightly that it becomes even more closely related to space. In fact, time simply becomes another dimension of space. According to Stephen's new reasoning, the beginning of the universe was not really a singularity—a dimensionless point. It was more like a

fuzziness. This means that the universe has no bound-
aries in time or space—no real beginning.

Does this mean that there was no big bang after all?
The situation gets even more complicated. To develop
his equations, Stephen had made use of a mathematical concept known as imaginary time. Here the word
imaginary does not mean "make-believe," as it usually
does. It is simply a different way of looking at time.
In imaginary time, the universe had no beginning.
However, we live in a dimension of time called real
time. Here's what Stephen has to say about it: "I still
believe the universe has a beginning in real time, at a
big bang. But there's another kind of time, imaginary
time, at right angles to real time, in which the universe has no beginning or end." Stephen liked this
solution because it upheld the laws of physics. No one
could say that these laws broke down prior to the big
bang. The laws of physics could still be considered
absolute and eternal.

STEPHEN AT THE VATICAN

Stephen knew the no boundary proposal would be
considered controversial. There was no way of proving whether his idea was correct or not. He also
feared some religious leaders might not like it. The
big bang theory seems to support the account of
creation given in the book of Genesis in the Bible.
Some people think that the no boundary proposal
does not. Despite the controversy he foresaw,

Stephen made a daring decision. He would present his new ideas at a conference on cosmology that was being held by the Vatican. Pope John Paul II would listen to Stephen's paper.

Because the new theory was so technical, it's possible that the pope did not understand everything that Stephen was trying to say. Later, Stephen said that he thought that was for the best. But George Coyne, a Jesuit priest and director of the Vatican Observatory, certainly understood Stephen's talk. Coyne was not alarmed or offended by anything that Stephen had to say. He didn't think it contradicted Christian beliefs, and he thought Stephen had completed a fine piece of work.

Stephen knew that the no boundary proposal did not present the whole story. "Although science may solve the problem of how the universe began," he said later, "it cannot answer the question: Why does the universe bother to exist? I don't know the answer to that."

Toward the end of the conference, everyone was introduced to Pope John Paul. The pope remained seated to greet most of the guests, but he knelt down by Stephen's wheelchair so they could face each other more easily. They spent quite a while in quiet conversation.

During the next year, Stephen visited Santa Barbara, California, to work with physicist James Hartle. Together they developed the mathematical details of the no boundary proposal. In 1983 they published their work.

Lucy (left), *Stephen* (sitting), *Robert* (standing), *Tim, and Jane Hawking* (right) *at their home*

SCIENCE IS FOR EVERYONE

Although Stephen was severely limited physically, his disease had leveled off and he was no longer getting worse. He tried not to look too far into his own future, but he worried about his children. Robert was fourteen years old. Lucy was almost eleven. It was time to start thinking about their education. Stephen wanted them to attend good schools, but he needed money for their tuition. He also realized that he would eventually need more money for his own medical care.

A friend of Stephen's, radio astronomer Simon Mitton, had been suggesting that he write a book. Stephen had already written academic books for fellow scientists, but Mitton had a broader audience in mind. Stephen began to consider the idea seriously. If he could make a lot of money on a popular book, his problems would be solved. But there was another reason the project appealed to Stephen. He felt everyone had the right to know what was happening in science. "I wanted to explain how far I felt we had come in our understanding of the universe," he said, "how we might be near finding a complete theory that would describe the universe and everything in it." The subject matter was difficult, but Stephen planned to present cosmology as a great adventure. He was determined to write a best seller.

Stephen had to overcome many obstacles to write A Brief
History of Time.

Chapter **SEVEN**

A NEW VOICE

WHIPPING UP A BEST SELLER PROVED TO BE MORE challenging than Stephen expected. "It's still far too technical," said Simon Mitton, after reading part of the book for the second time. "Look at it this way, Steve—every equation will halve your sales."

That made Stephen pause. He had equations on almost every page. If he wanted to make money, he had lots of editing to do. A literary agent helped him submit his proposal to U.S. publishers. Stephen decided to publish with Bantam Books. The company didn't specialize in science, but it had an enormous market. As Stephen noted, "[Bantam's] books were widely available in airport book stalls." That was good enough for him.

Stephen wrote and rewrote. He talked about the

history of science, the expanding universe, and Einstein's theory of general relativity. He also talked about the possibility of a grand theory of everything, which would explain all the phenomena in the universe. Of course, he explained how he developed his amazing ideas about black holes. It wouldn't be easy reading for the general public. It wasn't easy writing for Stephen either. He assumed that his readers would know certain basic facts about cosmology. Peter Guzzardi, his editor, assured him this wasn't so. He kept after Stephen to simplify things. Sometimes he asked Stephen to explain a concept more fully. "At times I thought the process would never end," recalled Stephen. But he was grateful for Guzzardi's help and knew he would have a stronger book.

HEALTH CRISIS

Stephen was still working on the manuscript when he decided to visit a research facility in Geneva, Switzerland, that was studying nuclear particles. New discoveries about elementary particles were being made there, and Stephen wanted to share the excitement firsthand. While Jane traveled in Germany, a nurse looked after Stephen in Switzerland. One night, when the nurse checked on Stephen, she found him gasping for breath. His face had turned purple. Stephen was rushed to the hospital and put on life support.

Stephen had pneumonia, a disease that can prove deadly for people with his condition. A distraught

Jane arrived as soon as she heard the news. Unable to breathe on his own, an unconscious Stephen was hooked up to a ventilator, a machine that would breathe for him. For the moment, he was stable. But doctors feared that an ALS patient would never fully recover from pneumonia and would face unbearable physical hardships. One of the doctors asked Jane if Stephen should be removed from the ventilator while he was still unconscious.

Jane was horrified. "Stephen must live!" she cried. "You must bring him out of the anaesthetic." Jane made sure that everything possible was done to ensure his survival. When Stephen regained consciousness, an air ambulance flew him back to England, where he entered the hospital in Cambridge. Finally, doctors performed a tracheotomy on him. A special tube was inserted into his neck so he could breathe without a ventilator. But this meant that Stephen would never speak again.

After the surgery, Stephen needed someone with him around the clock. The Hawkings didn't know how they would pay for the home care. But Jane was determined to hold the family together. As far as she was concerned, placing Stephen in a nursing facility was out of the question. She began contacting charitable organizations for help. Several responded favorably. The Hawkings received enough money to pay for the nursing care that Stephen needed.

Stephen's speech had been slurred and slow. But

those who knew him best could usually decipher what he was trying to say. Without a voice, he couldn't talk to his children. He couldn't finish his book. The only way Stephen could communicate was by lifting his eyebrows when someone pointed to the correct letter on an alphabet card. Letter by letter, Stephen could build up words and sentences. But the process took so long that meaningful conversation was almost impossible. He began to wonder if his life was worthwhile after all.

A LIFELINE

News of Stephen's plight spread throughout the scientific community. American computer expert Walt Woltosz had developed a computer program called Equalizer for his mother-in-law, who could not speak either. He sent Stephen a copy of the program. It would allow Stephen to use the slight movement that remained in his hand to select letters and common words on the computer screen. When he completed what he wanted to say, he could save it on a disk or he could send it to a speech synthesizer. The synthesizer would speak the words for him electronically.

At first, Stephen was reluctant to use the new computer program. Accepting it meant accepting that he would never speak naturally again. But Stephen had too much to say and do to remain silent. One evening he signaled to his research fellow Brian Whitt that he would like to try the computer. "Hello," Stephen greeted his assistant in his new artificial voice. Then he got down to business. "Will you help me finish my book?"

The Equalizer proved to be just the lifeline that Stephen needed. For the first time in many years, everyone knew what he was saying—even six-year-old Timothy who had never learned to understand his father's speech. "It was a bit slow," Stephen has said of his voice synthesizer, "but then I think slowly, so it suited me quite well." David Mason, a computer expert, was able to equip Stephen's wheelchair with a minicomputer and a voice synthesizer. Wherever he went, Stephen could talk with those around him. He liked to joke that his new voice had an American accent. Although it is artificial, it does have the normal inflections of everyday speech. It is also a gentle

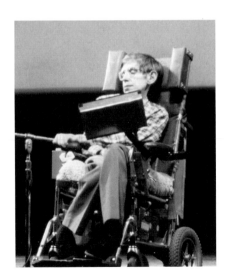

Stephen in his chair equipped with a minicomputer and voice synthesizer

and thoughtful voice that the *Washington Post* has called "oddly comforting."

CELEBRATING *A BRIEF HISTORY OF TIME*

Soon Stephen was back at work on his book. He thought he might include a special appendix with many of the mathematical equations he had omitted from the text. His editor nixed the suggestion at once. "It would terrify people!" he exclaimed. Stephen was also concerned about the book's title. He had decided on *A Brief History of Time*, but he worried about the word *brief.* He thought it might be too silly to use in a book about the beginning of the universe.

Once again, Peter Guzzardi disagreed with Stephen. He thought that the title was fantastic. He told Stephen that he smiled when he saw the word *brief.* That settled the matter for Stephen. A little humor never hurt anything. Besides, as Guzzardi has pointed out, "[Stephen] likes to make people smile."

In spring 1988, *A Brief History of Time* was published at last. Stephen and Jane went to New York to celebrate the occasion. A banquet was held in Stephen's honor. Afterward, Stephen went outside with his guests to look down on the East River. He was charged with energy and eager to chat with everyone. When he returned to his hotel, he heard music wafting down the hall. Stephen followed the sound to the ballroom where a dance was being held. It didn't matter that he hadn't been invited. Soon he was spinning around the dance floor in his wheelchair. Even when the party was officially over, the band continued to play just for him. He didn't stop dancing until early the next morning.

A Happy Surprise

Stephen had high hopes for his book, but some people at Bantam Books were a little nervous. They worried that the public might not be as interested in black holes and the big bang as Bantam had hoped. After all, these ideas were far removed from the practical concerns of everyday life. Would people be confused or intrigued by Stephen's explanation of the no boundary proposal? To be on the safe side, Bantam reduced the number of copies to be printed. The company didn't want to risk being stuck with lots of unsold books.

The publisher needn't have worried. In record time, bookstores sold out of *A Brief History of Time*. Perhaps it was the intriguing title or general admiration for Stephen and his accomplishments. Or perhaps, as Stephen had always suspected, most people are fascinated by cosmology. Whatever the reason, the books had flown off the shelves. Booksellers weren't worried about the printing mistake. Eagerly booksellers ordered new copies. Stephen Hawking had a runaway hit.

Stephen's success as a popular author made him the best-known scientist since Einstein.

Chapter EIGHT

GLOBE-TROTTING PHYSICIST

WITHIN MONTHS, SALES OF **A BRIEF HISTORY OF**
Time topped the one-million mark. Several months
after the appearance of the U.S. edition, the book was
published in Great Britain. In a matter of days, every
single copy was sold. The printers could not keep up
with the demand. Not everyone who bought Stephen's
book made it through to the end. But his final sen-
tence became famous. Stephen said that if a complete
theory of everything were discovered, scientists and
nonscientists alike would be better able to discuss
why the universe and human beings exist. "If we find
the answer to that, it would be the ultimate triumph
of human reason," Stephen concluded, "for then we
would know the mind of God."

Regardless of a person's religion, the thought of understanding the mind of God was intriguing Stephen seemed to be saying that there was no limit to what the human intellect could accomplish. Even more inspiring to some readers, Stephen's own life seemed to prove that there was no limit to what the human spirit could achieve. Stephen became a public hero. Wherever he went, people greeted him enthusiastically. His son Timothy was a little embarrassed by all the fuss, but Stephen enjoyed it greatly. "I am pleased a book on science competes with memoirs of pop stars," he joked in an interview with the *Cambridge Daily News*. "Maybe there is still hope for the human race."

HEAPED WITH HONORS

Journalists clamored for interviews with the most popular scientist since Einstein. A British film documentary, *Master of the Universe*, highlighted Stephen's life and work. In the United States, the television series *20/20* aired an interview with Stephen. Meanwhile, lecture requests poured in from all over the world. Stephen visited Japan, where hundreds of people lined up for each of his lectures. In January 1989, he went to Jerusalem, Israel, to accept a prestigious physics prize from the Wolf Foundation, an organization that honors outstanding scientists and artists. Stephen shared the prize with Roger Penrose for their work on black holes. Politicians and scientists from around the world attended the event, which was held in the Knesset, Israel's Parliament. That same year, Britain's queen Elizabeth II named Stephen a Companion of Honor, a distinction reserved for the most outstanding men and women in Great Britain. Stephen traveled to Buckingham Palace to receive the award from the queen.

More pomp and circumstance awaited him in Cambridge. The university broke with tradition by granting Stephen an honorary doctorate. Normally it did not bestow degrees on members of its own faculty. But there had never been an individual like Stephen. His contributions to physics and to the public understanding of science demanded to be acknowledged. Music from the college choirs and a brass ensemble filled the air as Stephen drove his wheelchair in the academic procession. Hundreds of people turned out to applaud him. On Saturday night, a Cambridge musical group performed a special concert downtown to honor Stephen. Afterward, he was brought onstage. Many men and women had tears in their eyes as they rose to applaud Stephen's accomplishments.

A Satisfying Life

Stephen had work he loved, a wonderful family, and the opportunity to exchange ideas with scientists all over the world. "One really can't ask for more," Stephen said of his life. But Jane worried about all the fuss and media attention. Stephen's frequent trips left him less time for his family. Robert and Lucy were already grown, but Timothy was only eleven. Jane felt that she couldn't leave him to travel with Stephen. She also had teaching commitments. "I cannot keep up with him," she said. "I do think he tends to overcompensate for his condition by doing absolutely everything that comes to his notice."

Stephen's high public profile made it easier for him to fight for the rights of disabled individuals. He helped raise money to create special living quarters for disabled students at Cambridge. He also worked to get a dormitory established for disabled students at Bristol University in Bristol, England. In gratitude for his help, officials named the new structure Hawking House. Stephen's own determination and courage gave many people a new awareness of what it meant to have a disability. Nothing could keep him down—not even an accident. One evening in 1991, Stephen was coming home in the rain. Suddenly he heard the screech of tires and his nurse shouting, "Look out!" A car plowed into the wheelchair, and Stephen was thrown into the road. He broke his arm and suffered serious cuts on his head. Doctors advised Stephen to take his time recovering. But two days later, Stephen was back at work with his books and papers propped up before him.

A BRIEF HISTORY OF TIME: THE MOVIE

Before the accident, Stephen was already busy with the movie version of his best-selling book. At first he had been dubious about the film project. He had wanted a documentary that would focus almost entirely on physics and cosmology. But director Errol Morris wanted lots of material on Stephen's life, including interviews with family and colleagues. He explained that a strictly scientific film wouldn't attract as many viewers. As Stephen became more involved, he learned to trust Morris and his instincts.

Morris carefully re-created every last detail of Stephen's office in the movie studio, including a poster of Marilyn Monroe. Morris was curious about

This image from the movie A Brief History of Time shows the picture of Marilyn Monroe hanging behind Hawking (left) and director Errol Morris.

that poster. Stephen said that he had liked the actress in the movie *Some Like It Hot*. Family and friends tended to remember that when buying him presents. He had a whole collection of Marilyn Monroe souvenirs. "I suppose you could say she was a model of the universe," Stephen quipped to Morris. He spent many hours under the bright camera lights explaining his theories in his calm, computer voice.

Filming for the movie coincided with a difficult time in Stephen's life. By the time the interviews were complete, Stephen and Jane had separated after almost twenty-five years of marriage. Friends and colleagues all over the world reacted with shock and dismay. Stephen's marriage had given him strength and comfort. According to news reporters who visited him at this time, he rarely smiled.

STRANGE IDEAS

Stephen used work to escape from the pain and confusion in his personal life. He still hoped to discover a theory of everything. In the meantime, Stephen came up with some very strange ideas. For example, he thought about the particles, objects (or even spaceships!) that might drop into a black hole. According to his theory, the black hole would explode and disappear someday. If it did, what would happen to the things that had fallen inside?

Stephen's answer was astounding. He believed that what fell into a black hole would branch off into a separate baby universe. Once again, Stephen had to resort to imaginary time to develop his idea. The baby universes can only exist in imaginary time. In real time, if an astronaut fell into a black hole, he would be destroyed by the tremendous gravity. Stephen said he would be stretched out like an infinitely long strand of spaghetti and torn apart. But in imaginary time, something of the astronaut continues to exist.

Stephen was concerned with ideas about the direction of time. He wondered what would happen if the expansion of the universe reversed itself. The galaxies would no longer be moving farther apart but would draw closer together. Did this mean that time would reverse itself too? For a while, Stephen thought so, even though the results seemed nonsensical. People in a collapsing universe would live their lives backward if Stephen were right. "Would we see broken cups gather themselves together off the floor and jump back onto the table?" he asked. Stephen set his graduate student Raymond LaFlamme to work on solving the problem.

But LaFlamme and Stephen's friend and colleague Don Page could not agree with him. "I had made a mistake," Stephen admitted in the film of *A Brief History of Time*. Then he couldn't resist a bit of fun at his own expense. "People will continue to get older, so it's no good waiting until the universe collapses to return to our youth."

IN HIS OWN WORDS

Stephen seized every opportunity that came his way. He traveled, lectured, and made his enthusiastic acting debut in *Star Trek*. "I don't regard myself as cut off from normal life," he told a radio broadcaster on Christmas Day 1992. "And I don't think people around me would say I was. . . . I suppose my life can hardly be described as usual, but I feel it is normal in spirit."

Stephen didn't feel that his intellect separated him from ordinary people either. He bristled at the very word *genius*. Once Stephen was asked how it felt to be considered "the smartest person in the world." Words flashed rapidly across his computer screen as he readied his reply. "It is very embarrassing," said the synthetic voice. "It is rubbish, just media hype. They

Stephen's computer screen shows his reflection. His computer is Stephen's main way of communicating with the world.

just want a hero, and I fit the role model of a disabled genius. At least, I am disabled, but I am not a genius."

Thirty years had passed since Stephen was given only two years to live. He is one of the world's most famous and beloved scientists. In 1993 his new book, *Black Holes and Baby Universes and Other Essays,* gave readers a glimpse into his personal life as well as his science. From his struggles with ALS to the probability that a huge black hole exists at the heart of the Milky Way, Stephen's text was riveting and easy to follow. Once again, he hit the best-seller charts.

People just couldn't get enough of Stephen. Sometimes U.S. tourists in Cambridge would spy him passing by in his wheelchair. "Stephen Hawking!" they'd call out. "I'm always being mistaken for that man," he'd joke in reply. His lectures drew hordes of non-scientists. When Stephen lectured in London, the five-thousand-seat Royal Albert Hall filled up with fans. It was the most popular physics lecture in Great Britain since Einstein had spoken at the same auditorium. The event was to raise money for a charity that dealt with motor neuron disease research, and Stephen waived his speaker's fee. He talked about black holes and what might happen to particles that fall inside. As for what discoveries the future might hold, Stephen Hawking could only conclude, "God still has a few tricks up his sleeve."

Stephen married Elaine Mason in September 1995.

Chapter **NINE**

A GLORIOUS TIME TO BE ALIVE

FOR THE PAST FEW YEARS, STEPHEN HAD OFTEN BEEN accompanied on his travels by his nurse and friend, Elaine Mason. Stephen came to depend on Elaine for emotional as well as nursing support. As Jane and Stephen grew apart, Stephen felt more and more drawn to Elaine. Finally, his feelings grew so strong that he felt he had to end his marriage to Jane. Stephen and Elaine were married in 1995.

Although his two oldest children were grown, Stephen did his best to remain a supportive, involved father to Robert, Lucy, and Timothy. Lucy was touched by the way her father always managed to surprise her with gifts of perfectly fitting clothes. "It means more to me that he knows what size I am, and not just what size galaxies are," she said. Stephen also enjoyed attending races and rock concerts with his son Tim. He once spoke on a radio show of his need for strong family bonds and friendship. "I couldn't carry on with my life if I only had physics," he admitted.

Fame had opened many opportunities to Stephen. On March 6, 1998, he presented a science lecture at the White House as part of a series called Millennium Evenings. Stephen gave an overview of important developments in physics and biology and his view of the future. U.S. president Bill Clinton called him "a genuine living miracle because of the power of the heart and the spirit."

Stephen felt perfectly at home from the White House to Hollywood. The next year, he made a guest appearance on the animated television show, *The Simpsons*. Enjoying his funny lines, he complimented Homer Simpson for his idea that the universe is shaped like a donut. The first successful appearance on *The Simpsons* led to others.

Because he was constantly on the go, Stephen felt he needed an even better wheelchair. In 2001 a husband-and-wife team from the United States delivered and fine-tuned his new Quantum Jazzy 1400 Power Chair. The woman, Terri Rozaieski, who was expecting her first child, was also wheelchair bound. Stephen waited for just the right moment to speak to her from his heart. "It might seem awkward being a disabled parent," he told her, "but I did not find it so. Children accept as natural that you are in a wheelchair. Ask for their help. Don't worry. Just make them part of the family team." His caring words meant a great deal to the expectant mother.

Stephen brainstormed names for his new chair. "Hawky's Comet," "Wormhole," and "Thunderbolt" were among the contenders. His personalized license plate reads T4SWH, which stands for Tea for Stephen William Hawking. It's a drink he loves.

Stephen put his new power chair to work when he went to Germany to launch his new book, which had the catchy title *The Universe in a Nutshell*. Although it covers some of the same material as *A Brief History of Time*, it goes far beyond it. Aimed once again at a popular audience, the new book discusses such topics as the possibility of time travel and the *Star Trek* vision

A new power chair enables Stephen to travel more easily. Here he delivers a speech, "The Origin of the Universe," in Germany.

of the future. The book makes the point that, although humans have all sorts of physical limitations, there are no limits to our imagination. Our minds can take us anywhere in the universe.

Once again, Stephen's writing proved popular. In June 2002, he received the Aventis Book Prize, an award managed by the Royal Society and Great Britain's National Academy of Science. Sponsored by the Aventis Pharmaceutical Company, the prize is given to books that best explain science to the general public. "Wherever I go around the world, people want to know more," Stephen declared on accepting the award.

HAPPY BIRTHDAY, STEPHEN

On January 8, 2002, Stephen celebrated his sixtieth birthday. Scientists came to Cambridge from all over the world to greet him and participate in a special birthday conference. Some of them gave talks about cosmology. Scientist Leonard Susskind called Stephen "one of the most obstinate people in the world; no he is the most infuriating person in the universe." Seated toward the back of the room, Stephen flashed his famous grin. Another cheerful note was his friend Kip Thorne's promise that by the time Stephen turned seventy, all his theories about black holes would have been tested.

Then the audience grew very silent. It was time for Stephen himself to speak. "It has been a glorious time to be alive, and doing research in theoretical physics. Our picture of the universe has changed a great deal

Stephen smiles at his sixtieth birthday conference.

in the last forty years, and I'm happy if I have made a small contribution. I want to share my excitement and enthusiasm. There's nothing like the Eureka moment of discovering something that no one knew before."

TURNABOUT

But sometimes such moments can work in reverse. Two and a half years later, in July 2004, newspaper headlines proclaimed, "Hawking admits being wrong." At a jammed conference in Dublin, Ireland, Stephen explained that he no longer believed that black holes totally destroy everything that falls inside. Some information, he declared, might be returned to the universe. Stephen said he had been thinking about the problem for thirty years. His new theory meant also revising his previous ideas about baby universes branching out from black holes. "I'm sorry to disappoint science fiction fans," he said. "But if information is preserved, there is no possibility of using black holes to travel to other universes. If you jump into a black hole, your mass energy will be returned to our Universe but in a mangled form."

All over the world, scientists discussed Stephen's new views. But John Preskill, a physicist at Caltech, was especially pleased with Stephen's turnabout. Preskill had bet Stephen and Kip Thorne that information falling into a black hole was NOT lost forever. It was time for Stephen to pay up. He gave Preskill a book titled *Total Baseball*. Preskill gladly accepted his prize but admitted afterward, "I'll be honest, I didn't understand [Stephen's] talk." He was eager to study the paper that Stephen planned to publish.

As for Stephen, he didn't mind admitting an error, though he had had to search long and hard to find a book on baseball in England. "Do you feel that scientists correct themselves as often as they should?" a reporter asked him early in 2005. "More often than politicians, but not as often as they should," replied Stephen. As usual, he had managed to combine honesty and humor in the fewest number of words.

Still Curious

Through his writing, Stephen had awakened many people to the wonder of cosmology. But he felt that *A*

Brief History of Time was too difficult for many readers. Stephen still wanted to reach the broadest audience possible. So he wrote a simpler book. He called it *A Briefer History of Time*. He also developed and played himself in a movie on the universe, *Beyond the Horizon*. Written for a popular audience, it aims to show that cosmology is relevant to our lives and to the way we view our place in the universe.

Stephen had to change his prediction that the theory of everything would be found before the end of the twentieth century. But he remains hopeful that scientists are close to finding the ultimate secrets of the universe. And he continues to take great joy in his work. Even if a theory of everything is discovered, that will not mean the end of physics or the end of Stephen's work.

On Christmas Day 1999, talk show host Larry King interviewed Stephen on the CNN network. At the end of the program, he asked his guest what keeps him going. Stephen said his secret lay in his boundless curiosity. He had so many questions, and he wanted to find the answers. Stephen told Larry King that he loved life and that he planned to keep working as long as possible. Because he always refused to quit, Stephen has vastly increased our knowledge of the universe. His accomplishments have made him an inspiration to people all over the world.

GLOSSARY

atom: the smallest identifiable unit of any chemical element

big bang: the theory that the entire universe (including matter, space, and time) burst into existence from a singularity

binary system: a pair of stars that revolve around one another

black hole: an object whose gravity is so great that nothing—not even light—can escape its pull. A black hole forms when a large star collapses in on itself.

cosmology: the study of the cosmos, or universe

Cygnus X-1: the first black hole identified in outer space

density: the amount of substance or matter in a given volume

electron: a negatively charged particle that orbits the center (nucleus) of an atom

entropy: a measure of the amount of disorder in a system

event horizon: the boundary of a black hole where light is trapped and cannot escape back into space

gravity: a property of matter and space that causes objects to be attracted to one another

Hawking radiation: virtual particles at the edge of a black hole that become real and seem to radiate into space

imaginary time: time measured using imaginary numbers

neutron star: a collapsed star that may contain millions of tons of matter for each cubic inch

no boundary proposal: the idea that the same laws of physics hold everywhere in space and time, including at the very beginning of the universe

particle physics: the science of the subatomic particles that make up all matter; also called quantum physics

photon: a particle of light

physics, classical: physics based on principles developed before the rise of quantum theory

proton: a positively charged particle found in the center (nucleus) of an atom

pulsar: a rotating neutron star that gives off regularly spaced pulses of radiation

quantum fluctuation: a spontaneous temporary change in the amount of energy present in a point in space

radiation: energy in the form of waves or particles

relativity, general theory of: the theory developed by Albert Einstein that explains gravity as curvature of space around large bodies like the Sun or the planets

singularity: a mathematical point without dimensions where the laws of physics break down

steady state theory: the theory that the universe has always existed and always will

theory of everything: a single theory to account for everything that happens in the universe

uncertainty principle: a rule of quantum physics that limits what can be known about a subatomic particle

virtual particle: a pair of particles (one positive and one negative) that appear spontaneously through a quantum fluctuation in outer space and annihilate one another

white dwarf: a partially collapsed star in which hundreds of tons of matter are packed within each cubic inch

SOURCES

11 Stephen Hawking, *Black Holes and Baby Universes and Other Essays* (New York: Bantam Books, 1993), 1.

16 Hawking, *Black Holes and Baby Universes*, 7.

16 Hawking, Stephen Hawking, ed., *Stephen Hawking's A Brief History of Time: A Reader's Companion, prepared by Gene Stone*, (New York: Bantam Books, 1992), 11.

18–19 Hawking, *Black Holes and Baby Universes*, 5.

19 Michael White and John Gribbin, *Stephen Hawking: A Life in Science* (Washington D.C.: Joseph Henry Press, 2002), 20.

20 Hawking, *Black Holes and Baby Universes*, 11.

25 David Filkin, *Stephen Hawking's Universe: The Cosmos Explained*. With a foreword by Stephen Hawking, (New York: Basic Books, 1997). 4.

26 Hawking, *A Reader's Companion*, 165

27 Kitty Ferguson, *Stephen Hawking: Quest for a Theory of Everything* (New York: Bantam Books, 1991), 39.

33 Hawking, *Black Holes and Baby Universes*, 22.

34 Jane Hawking, *Music to Move the Stars: A Life with Stephen* (London: Pan Books, 2000), 46.

35 Hawking, *Black Holes and Baby Universes*, 23.

38 J. P. McEvoy and Oscar Zarate, *Introducing Stephen Hawking* (London: Icon Books, 1995), 71.

38 Ibid.

41 Alan Lightman and Roberta Brawer, *Origins: The Lives and Worlds of Modern Cosmologists* (Cambridge, MA: Harvard University Press, 1990), 145.

42 Hawking, *Black Holes and Baby Universes*, 16.

45 Ferguson, 46.

51 John Boslough, *Stephen Hawking's Universe: An Introduction to the Most Remarkable Scientist of Our Time* (New York: Avon Books, 1985), 46.

53 Jerry Adler, Gerald C. Lubenow, and Maggie Malone, "Reading God's Mind," *Newsweek*, June 13, 1988, quoted in White and Gribbin, 117.

54   Dennis Overbye, *Lonely Hearts of the Cosmos: The Story of the Scientific Quest for the Secret of the Universe* (Boston: Little, Brown and Company, 1991), 100.

58   White and Gribbin, 130.

59   Ibid., 83.

59   Hawking, *Black Holes and Baby Universes*, 120.

59   White and Gribbin, 131.

63   Ibid, 157.

64   Ferguson, 88.

65   Ibid., 90.

65   Overbye, 117.

66   Ibid.

67   Hawking, *Black Holes and Baby Universes*, 68.

69   White and Gribbin, 196.

69   Ibid.

70   Ibid., 197.

70   "The Sky's No Limit in the Career of Stephen Hawking," *West Australian*, 1989, quoted in White and Gribbin, 194.

72   Hawking, *Black Holes and Baby Universes*, 172.

73   Ibid., 99.

75   Ibid., 34.

77   White and Gribbin, 223.

77   Hawking, *Black Holes and Baby Universes*, 34.

78   Ibid., 35.

79   Jane Hawking, 435.

81   Hawking, *A Reader's Companion*, 155.

81   White and Gribbin, 236.

82   Linton Weeks, "In Hawking, Smithsonian Honors a True Mr. Universe," *Washington Post*, February 15, 2005.

82   White and Gribbin, 237.

82   Ibid., 241.

82   Ibid.

85   Hawking, *The Illustrated A Brief History of Time*, rev. ed. (New York: Bantam Books, 1996), 233.

86   White and Gribbin, 245.

87   Ferguson, 158.

88   Ibid., 157.

90   White and Gribbin, 283.

91   Hawking, *A Reader's Companion*, 163.

91   Ibid., 167.
92   Hawking, *Black Holes and Baby Universes*, 158.
92–93   Lisa Kremer, "The Smartest Person in the World Refuses to Be Trapped by Fate," *Morning News Tribune*, July 2, 1993, also available online at *University of Washington*, January 31, 2002, http://www.washington.edu/doit/ Press/hawking3.html (June 8, 2005).
93   Robin McKie, "The Observer Profile: Stephen Hawking; Master of the Universe," *Guardian Unlimited*, October 21, 2001, http://education.guardian.co.uk/academicexerts/ comment/0,1392,578601,00.html (June 8, 2005).
93   White and Gribbin, 309.
95–96   McKie, "The Observer Profile."
96   Hawking, *Black Holes and Baby Universes*, 159.
96   "Remarks by President Clinton and Q&As at Hawking Lecture," *The White House Millennium Council*, 2000, http://clinton4.nara.gov/Initiatives/Millennium/19980309- 22774.html (May 16, 2005).
96–97   Terri Rozaieski, "Visiting with Dr. Stephen Hawking," *Pride Web Talk*, http://www.pridemobility.com/ pridewebtalk/Stephen_Hawking/stephen_hawking.html (December 28, 2004).
98   "Archive 2002–2004," *Stephen Hawking*, July 2002, http:// www.hawking.org.uk/info/iindex.html (January 24, 2005).
98   Dennis Overbye, "Hawking's Breakthrough Is Still an Enigma," *New York Times*, January 22, 2002, http://www.plambeck.org/oldhtml/journal/susskind/Single PageVersionHawking.htm (January 14, 2005).
98–99   Stephen Hawking, "Stephen Hawking's 60 years in a Nutshell," 1997–2004 Millennium Mathmatics Project, University of Cambridge, January 2002, http://plus.maths .org/issue18/features/hawking/index.html (February 2, 2005).
100   Jenny Hogan, "Hawking Concedes Black Hole Bet," *NewScientist.com*, July 21, 2004, http://www.newscientist .com/articlens?id=dn6193 (June 8, 2005).
100   Associated Press, "Hawking Unveils New Thinking on Black Holes," MSNBC.com, July 21, 2004, http://www.msnbc .msn.com/id/5473323/print/1/dispalymode/1098 (January 23, 2005).

100   New York Times Syndicate, Deborah Solomon, "A Chat with Stephen Hawking," *San Diego Union-Tribune,* January 2005, http://www.signonsandiego.com/uniontrib/20050112/news_1c12hawking.html (January 23, 2005).

SELECTED BIBLIOGRAPHY

Boslough, John. *Stephen Hawking's Universe: An Introduction to the Most Remarkable Scientist of Our Time.* New York: Avon Books, 1985.

Ferguson, Kitty. *Stephen Hawking: Quest for a Theory of Everything.* New York: Bantam Books, 1991.

Filkin, David. *Stephen Hawking's Universe: The Cosmos Explained.* Foreword by Stephen Hawking. New York: Basic Books, 1997.

Hawking, Jane. *Music to Move the Stars: A Life with Stephen Hawking.* London: Pan Books, 2000.

Hawking, Stephen. *Black Holes and Baby Universes and Other Essays.* New York: Bantam Books, 1993.

_____. *The Illustrated A Brief History of Time*, Rev. ed. New York: Bantam Books, 1996.

_____ed. *Stephen Hawking's A Brief History of Time: A Reader's Companion.* Prepared by Gene Stone. New York: Bantam Books, 1992.

_____. *The Universe in a Nutshell.* New York: Bantam Books, 2001.

McEvoy, J. P., and Oscar Zarate. *Introducing Stephen Hawking.* London: Icon Books, 1995

White, Michael, and John Gribbin. *Stephen Hawking: A Life in Science.* Washington DC: Joseph Henry Press, 2002.

FURTHER READING AND WEBSITES

ALS Association Homepage
http://www.alsa.org/. This website provides information about ALS research, symptoms, and resources for those living with the disease, as wells as contact information for local chapters.

Couper, Heather, and Nigel Henbest, *How the Universe Works: 100 Ways Parents and Kids Can Share the Secrets of the Universe*, Pleasantville, NY: Reader's Digets, 1994.

Davis, Kenneth C. *Don't Know Much About Space.* New York: HarperCollins Children's Books, 1994.

Fleisher, Paul. *The Big Bang.* Minneapolis: Twenty-First Century Books, 2006.

_____. *Relativity and Quantum Mechanics.* Minneapolis: Twenty-First Century, 2002.

Professor Stephen Hawking's Homepage
http:// www.hawking.org.uk/home/hindex.html. This site contains a mini bio, discussion of Hawking's illness, and links.

Usborne Publishing. *The Usborne First Guide to the Universe,* London: Usborne Publishing, 1993.

WEBSITES

INDEX

OTHER TITLES FROM LERNER AND BIOGRAPHY®:

Ariel Sharon
Arnold Schwarzenegger
The Beatles
Benito Mussolini
Benjamin Franklin
Bill Gates
Billy Graham
Carl Sagan
Che Guevara
Chief Crazy Horse
Colin Powell
Daring Pirate Women
Edgar Allan Poe
Eleanor Roosevelt
Fidel Castro
Frank Gehry
George Lucas
George W. Bush
Gloria Estefan
Hillary Rodham Clinton
Jacques Cousteau
Jane Austen
Jesse Ventura
J. K. Rowling
Joseph Stalin
Latin Sensations

Legends of Dracula
Legends of Santa Claus
Malcolm X
Mao Zedong
Mark Twain
Maya Angelou
Mohandas Gandhi
Napoleon Bonaparte
Nelson Mandela
Osama bin Laden
Pope Benedict XVI
Queen Cleopatra
Queen Elizabeth I
Queen Latifah
Rosie O'Donnell
Saddam Hussein
Stephen Hawking
Thurgood Marshall
Tiger Woods
Tony Blair
Vladimir Putin
Wilma Rudolph
Winston Churchill
Women in Space
Women of the Wild West
Yasser Arafat

ABOUT THE AUTHOR

Stephanie Sammartino McPherson, a former journalist, enjoys writing about science for young people. Her children's books include "Ordinary Genius: The Story of Albert Einstein," "Jonas Salk: Conquering Polio," and "Wilbur and Orville Wright: Taking Flight" (written with her nephew Joseph Sammartino Gardner). Stephanie and her husband Richard live in Virginia but also call California home. They are the parents of two grown children.

PHOTO ACKNOWLEDGMENTS